I0845262

CHECK POINT CERTIFIED SECURITY EXPERT PRACTICE TEST AND DUMPS

Exam Prep Guide for CCSE

Published by:

Impact Books

Cover & Interior Designed By

By

Sharon Loxley

1st Edition

Impact Books: Empowering Minds, Changing Lives

At Impact Books, we believe in the transformative power of knowledge. We are not just a publisher; we are a catalyst for change, a platform that empowers minds, and a gateway to new perspectives. Our mission is to bring impactful non-fiction literature to the world, shaping lives and fostering growth through the written word.

Our journey began with a small team of dedicated individuals who shared a common dream: to provide a voice for writers whose stories and expertise could inspire and educate. Over the years, we have grown into a diverse family of authors, editors, designers, and collaborators united by our commitment to quality, integrity, and making a positive impact on readers worldwide.

QUESTION 1

What are the different command sources that allow you to communicate with the API server?
A. SmartView Monitor, API_cli Tool, Gaia CLI, Web Services
B. SmartConsole GUI Console, mgmt_cli Tool, Gaia CLI, Web Services
C. SmartConsole GUI Console, API_cli Tool, Gaia CLI, Web Services
D. API_cli Tool, Gaia CLI, Web Services

Reference:
 https://sc1.checkpoint.com/documents/R80/APIs/#introduction%20

QUESTION 2

What makes Anti-Bot unique compared to other Threat Prevention mechanisms, such as URL Filtering, Anti-Virus, IPS, and Threat Emulation?

A. Anti-Bot is the only countermeasure against unknown malware
B. Anti-Bot is the only protection mechanism which starts a counter-attack against known Command & Control Centers
C. Anti-Bot is the only signature-based method of malware protection.
D. Anti-Bot is a post-infection malware protection to prevent a host from establishing a connection to a Command & Control Center.

Reference:
 https://sc1.checkpoint.com/documents/R76/CP_R76_AntiBotAntiVirus_AdminGuide/index.html

QUESTION 3

Which TCP-port does CPM process listen to?

A. 18191
B. 18190
C. 8983
D. 19009

Reference:
https://www.checkpoint.com/downloads/products/r80.10-security-management-architecture-overview.pdf

QUESTION 4

Your manager asked you to check the status of SecureXL, and its enabled templates and features. What command will you use to provide such information to manager?

A. fw accel stat
B. fwaccel stat
C. fw acces stats
D. fwaccel stats

Reference:

https://supportcenter.checkpoint.com/supportcenter/portal?eventSubmit_doGoviewsolutiondetails=&solutionid=sk41397

QUESTION 5

SSL Network Extender (SNX) is a thin SSL VPN on-demand client that is installed on the remote user's machine via the web browser. What are the two modes of SNX?

A. Application and Client Service
B. Network and Application
C. Network and Layers
D. Virtual Adapter and Mobile App

Reference:

https://supportcenter.checkpoint.com/supportcenter/portal?eventSubmit_doGoviewsolutiondetails=&solutionid=sk67820

QUESTION 6

Which command would disable a Cluster Member permanently?

A. clusterXL_admin down
B. cphaprob_admin down
C. clusterXL_admin down-p
D. set clusterXL down-p

QUESTION 7

Fill in the blank: The tool_________generates a R80 Security Gateway configuration report.

A. `infoCP`
B. `infoview`
C. `cpinfo`
D. `fw cpinfo`

QUESTION 8

Automatic affinity means that if SecureXL is running, the affinity for each interface is automatically reset every

A. 15 sec
B. 60 sec
C. 5 sec
D. 30 sec

Reference:

https://sc1.checkpoint.com/documents/R76/CP_R76_PerformanceTuning_WebAdmin/6731.htm

QUESTION 9
Which command will allow you to see the interface status?

A. cphaprob interface
B. cphaprob –I interface
C. cphaprob –a if
D. cphaprob stat

Reference:

https://sc1.checkpoint.com/documents/R76/CP_R76_ClusterXL_AdminGuide/7298.htm

QUESTION 10
To help SmartEvent determine whether events originated internally or externally you must define using the Initial Settings under General Settings in the Policy Tab. How many options are available to calculate the traffic direction?

A. 5 Network; Host; Objects; Services; API
B. 3 Incoming; Outgoing; Network
C. 2 Internal; External
D. 4 Incoming; Outgoing; Internal; Other

Reference:

http://dl3.checkpoint.com/paid/21/CP_R76_SmartEventIntro_AdminGuide.pdf?HashKey=1538417023_7cb74dfe0
e109c21f130f556d419faaf&xtn=.pdf

QUESTION 11
You noticed that CPU cores on the Security Gateway are usually 100% utilized and many packets were dropped. You don't have a budget to perform a hardware upgrade at this time. To optimize drops you decide to use Priority Queues and fully enable Dynamic Dispatcher. How can you enable them?

A. fw ctl multik dynamic_dispatching on
B. fw ctl multik dynamic_dispatching set_mode 9
C. fw ctl multik set_mode 9
D. fw ctl multik pq enable

Reference:

https://supportcenter.checkpoint.com/supportcenter/portal?eventSubmit_doGoviewsolutiondetails=&solutionid=sk
105261

QUESTION 12
Which packet info is ignored with Session Rate Acceleration?

A. source port ranges
B. source ip
C. source port
D. same info from Packet Acceleration is used

Reference:

http://trlj.blogspot.com/2015/10/check-point-acceleration.html

QUESTION 13

Connections to the Check Point R80 Web API use what protocol?

A. HTTPS
B. SOAP
C. HTTP
D. SIC

QUESTION 14

What is true about the IPS-Blade?

A. In R80, IPS is managed by the Threat Prevention Policy
B. In R80, in the IPS Layer, the only three possible actions are Basic, Optimized and Strict
C. In R80, IPS Exceptions cannot be attached to "all rules"
D. In R80, the GeoPolicy Exceptions and the Threat Prevention Exceptions are the same

QUESTION 15

What Factor preclude Secure XL Templating?

A. Source Port Ranges/Encrypted Connections
B. IPS
C. ClusterXL in load sharing Mode
D. CoreXL

QUESTION 16

In order to get info about assignment (FW, SND) of all CPUs in your SGW, what is the most accurate CLI command?

A. fw ctl sdstat
B. fw ctl affinity –l –a –r –v
C. fw ctl multik stat
D. cpinfo

QUESTION 17

What is not a component of Check Point SandBlast?

A. Threat Emulation
B. Threat Simulator
C. Threat Extraction
D. Threat Cloud

QUESTION 18

Full synchronization between cluster members is handled by Firewall Kernel. Which port is used for this?

A. UDP port 265
B. TCP port 265
C. UDP port 256
D. TCP port 256

Explanation:

Synchronization works in two modes:
Full Sync transfers all Security Gateway kernel table information from one cluster member to another. It is handled by the fwd daemon using an encrypted TCP connection on port 256.
Delta Sync transfers changes in the kernel tables between cluster members. Delta sync is handled by the Security Gateway kernel using UDP connections on port 8116.

Reference:

https://sc1.checkpoint.com/documents/R80.10/WebAdminGuides/EN/CP_R80.10_ClusterXL_AdminGuide/html_fr ameset.htm?topic=documents/ R80.10/WebAdminGuides/EN/CP_R80.10_ClusterXL_AdminGuide/7288

QUESTION 19

Which of the following type of authentication on Mobile Access can NOT be used as the first authentication method?

A. Dynamic ID
B. RADIUS
C. Username and Password
D. Certificate

Reference:

https://sc1.checkpoint.com/documents/R80.10/WebAdminGuides/EN/CP_R80.10_MobileAccess_AdminGuide/ht ml_frameset.htm?topic=documents/
R80.10/WebAdminGuides/EN/CP_R80.10_MobileAccess_AdminGuide/41587

QUESTION 20

Which of the SecureXL templates are enabled by default on Security Gateway?

A. Accept
B. Drop
C. NAT
D. None

QUESTION 21

What happen when IPS profile is set in Detect Only Mode for troubleshooting?

A. It will generate Geo-Protection traffic
B. Automatically uploads debugging logs to Check Point Support Center
C. It will not block malicious traffic
D. Bypass licenses requirement for Geo-Protection control

Explanation:

It is recommended to enable Detect-Only for Troubleshooting on the profile during the initial installation of IPS.
This option overrides any protections that are set to Prevent so that they will not block any traffic.
During this time you can analyze the alerts that IPS generates to see how IPS will handle network traffic, while

avoiding any impact on the flow of traffic.

Reference:

https://sc1.checkpoint.com/documents/R76/CP_R76_IPS_AdminGuide/12750.htm

QUESTION 22

What is true about VRRP implementations?

A. VRRP membership is enabled in cpconfig
B. VRRP can be used together with ClusterXL, but with degraded performance
C. You cannot have a standalone deployment
D. You cannot have different VRIDs in the same physical network

Reference:

https://sc1.checkpoint.com/documents/R76/CP_R76_Gaia_WebAdmin/87911.htm

QUESTION 23

In a Client to Server scenario, which represents that the packet has already checked against the tables and the Rule Base?

A. Big I
B. Little o
C. Little i
D. Big O

QUESTION 24

What is the mechanism behind Threat Extraction?

A. This a new mechanism which extracts malicious files from a document to use it as a counter-attack against its sender.
B. This is a new mechanism which is able to collect malicious files out of any kind of file types to destroy it prior to sending it to the intended recipient.
C. This is a new mechanism to identify the IP address of the sender of malicious codes and put it into the SAM database (Suspicious Activity Monitoring).
D. Any active contents of a document, such as JavaScripts, macros and links will be removed from the document and forwarded to the intended recipient, which makes this solution very fast.

QUESTION 25

Which view is NOT a valid CPVIEW view?

A. IDA
B. DLP
C. PDP
D. VPN

QUESTION 26

Sticky Decision Function (SDF) is required to prevent which of the following? Assume you set up an Active-Active cluster.

A. Symmetric routing
B. Failovers
C. Asymmetric routing
D. Anti-Spoofing

QUESTION 27

If you needed the Multicast MAC address of a cluster, what command would you run?

A. cphaprob –a if
B. cphaconf ccp multicast
C. cphaconf debug data
D. cphaprob igmp

QUESTION 28

What are the three components for Check Point Capsule?

A. Capsule Docs, Capsule Cloud, Capsule Connect
B. Capsule Workspace, Capsule Cloud, Capsule Connect
C. Capsule Workspace, Capsule Docs, Capsule Connect
D. Capsule Workspace, Capsule Docs, Capsule Cloud

Reference:

https://www.checkpoint.com/products-solutions/mobile-security/check-point-capsule/

QUESTION 29

Which of the following Check Point processes within the Security Management Server is responsible for the receiving of log records from Security Gateway?

A. logd
B. fwd
C. fwm
D. cpd

Reference:

https://supportcenter.checkpoint.com/supportcenter/portal?eventSubmit_doGoviewsolutiondetails=&solutionid=sk97638

QUESTION 30

The Firewall Administrator is required to create 100 new host objects with different IP addresses. What API command can he use in the script to achieve the requirement?

A. add host name <New HostName> ip-address <ip address>
B. add hostname <New HostName> ip-address <ip address>
C. set host name <New HostName> ip-address <ip address>
D. set hostname <New HostName> ip-address <ip address>

Reference:

https://sc1.checkpoint.com/documents/R80/APIs/#intro_gui_cli%20

QUESTION 31

Tom has been tasked to install Check Point R80 in a distributed deployment. Before Tom installs the systems this way, how many machines will he need if he does NOT include a SmartConsole machine in his calculations?

A. One machine, but it needs to be installed using SecurePlatform for compatibility purposes.
B. One machine
C. Two machines
D. Three machines

Explanation:

One for Security Management Server and the other one for the Security Gateway.

QUESTION 32

When doing a Stand-Alone Installation, you would install the Security Management Server with which other Check Point architecture component?

A. None, Security Management Server would be installed by itself.
B. SmartConsole
C. SecureClient
D. SmartEvent

QUESTION 33

What is the least amount of CPU cores required to enable CoreXL?

A. 2
B. 1
C. 4
D. 6

Reference:

https://sc1.checkpoint.com/documents/R76/CP_R76_PerformanceTuning_WebAdmin/6731.htm

QUESTION 34

You are working with multiple Security Gateways enforcing an extensive number of rules. To simplify security administration, which action would you choose?

A. Eliminate all possible contradictory rules such as the Stealth or Cleanup rules.
B. Create a separate Security Policy package for each remote Security Gateway.
C. Create network objects that restricts all applicable rules to only certain networks.
D. Run separate SmartConsole instances to login and configure each Security Gateway directly.

QUESTION 35

Which of the following authentication methods ARE NOT used for Mobile Access?

A. RADIUS server
B. Username and password (internal, LDAP)
C. SecurID
D. TACACS+

Reference:
 https://sc1.checkpoint.com/documents/R77/CP_R77_Mobile_Access_WebAdmin/41587.htm

QUESTION 36

What is the correct command to observe the Sync traffic in a VRRP environment?

A. fw monitor –e "accept[12:4,b]=224.0.0.18;"
B. fw monitor –e "accept port(6118;"
C. fw monitor –e "accept proto=mcVRRP;"
D. fw monitor –e "accept dst=224.0.0.18;"

QUESTION 37

What are the attributes that SecureXL will check after the connection is allowed by Security Policy?

A. Source address, Destination address, Source port, Destination port, Protocol
B. Source MAC address, Destination MAC address, Source port, Destination port, Protocol
C. Source address, Destination address, Source port, Destination port
D. Source address, Destination address, Destination port, Protocol

QUESTION 38

Which statement is NOT TRUE about Delta synchronization?

A. Using UDP Multicast or Broadcast on port 8161
B. Using UDP Multicast or Broadcast on port 8116
C. Quicker than Full sync
D. Transfers changes in the Kernel tables between cluster members.

Reference:
https://sc1.checkpoint.com/documents/R76/CP_R76_ClusterXL_AdminGuide/7288.htm

QUESTION 39

In R80.10, how do you manage your Mobile Access Policy?

A. Through the Unified Policy
B. Through the Mobile Console
C. From SmartDashboard
D. From the Dedicated Mobility Tab

QUESTION 40

Which command can you use to verify the number of active concurrent connections?

A. fw conn all
B. fw ctl pstat
C. show all connections
D. show connections

Reference:

QUESTION 41

How can SmartView application accessed?

A. http://<Security Management IP Address>/smartview
B. http://<Security Management IP Address>:4434/smartview/
C. https://<Security Management IP Address>/smartview/
D. https://<Security Management host name>:4434/smartview/

QUESTION 42

In CoreXL, the Firewall kernel is replicated multiple times, therefore:

A. The Firewall kernel only touches the packet if the connection is accelerated
B. The Firewall can run different policies per core
C. The Firewall kernel is replicated only with new connections and deletes itself once the connection times out
D. The Firewall can run the same policy on all cores.

Explanation:

On a Security Gateway with CoreXL enabled, the Firewall kernel is replicated multiple times. Each replicated copy, or instance, runs on one processing core. These instances handle traffic concurrently, and each instance is a complete and independent inspection kernel. When CoreXL is enabled, all the kernel instances in the Security Gateway process traffic through the same interfaces and apply the same security policy.

Reference:
https://sc1.checkpoint.com/documents/R77/CP_R77_PerformanceTuning_WebAdmin/6731.htm

QUESTION 43

Advanced Security Checkups can be easily conducted within:

A. Reports
B. Advanced
C. Checkups
D. Views
E. Summary

QUESTION 44
Which of the following process pulls application monitoring status?

A. fwd
B. fwm
C. cpwd
D. cpd

QUESTION 45
To fully enable Dynamic Dispatcher on a Security Gateway:

A. run "fw ctl multik dynamic_dispatching on" and then Reboot.
B. Using cpconfig, update the Dynamic Dispatcher value to "full" under the CoreXL menu.
C. Edit/proc/interrupts to include multik set_mode 1 at the bottom of the file, save, and reboot.
D. run fw ctl multik set_mode 1 in Expert mode and then reboot.

QUESTION 46
Session unique identifiers are passed to the web api using which http header option?

A. X-chkp-sid
B. Accept-Charset
C. Proxy-Authorization
D. Application

QUESTION 47
What SmartEvent component creates events?

A. Consolidation Policy
B. Correlation Unit
C. SmartEvent Policy
D. SmartEvent GUI

Reference:

 https://sc1.checkpoint.com/documents/R76/CP_R76_SmartEvent_AdminGuide/17401.htm

QUESTION 48
Which features are only supported with R80.10 Gateways but not R77.x?

A. Access Control policy unifies the Firewall, Application Control & URL Filtering, Data Awareness, and Mobile
   Access Software Blade policies
B. Limits the upload and download throughput for streaming media in the company to 1 Gbps.
C. The rule base can be built of layers, each containing a set of the security rules. Layers are inspected in the
   order in which they are defined, allowing control over the rule base flow and which security functionalities take
   precedence.
D. Time object to a rule to make the rule active only during specified times.

Reference:

 http://slideplayer.com/slide/12183998/

QUESTION 49

Which CLI command will reset the IPS pattern matcher statistics?

A. ips reset pmstat
B. ips pstats reset
C. ips pmstats refresh
D. ips pmstats reset

Reference:

 https://sc1.checkpoint.com/documents/R76/CP_R76_CLI_WebAdmin/84627.htm

QUESTION 50
When requiring certificates for mobile devices, make sure the authentication method is set to one of the following,
Username and Password, RADIUS or_____________________

A. SecureID
B. SecurID
C. Complexity
D. TacAcs

Reference:
 https://sc1.checkpoint.com/documents/R77/CP_R77_Mobile_Access_WebAdmin/41587.htm

QUESTION 51

Check Point recommends configuring Disk Space Management parameters to delete old log entries when
available disk space is less than or equal to?

A. 50%
B. 75%
C. 80%
D. 15%

QUESTION 52

SecureXL improves non-encrypted firewall traffic throughput and encrypted VPN traffic throughput.

A. This statement is true because SecureXL does improve all traffic.
B. This statement is false because SecureXL does not improve this traffic but CoreXL does.
C. This statement is true because SecureXL does improve this traffic.
D. This statement is false because encrypted traffic cannot be inspected.

Explanation:
SecureXL improved non-encrypted firewall traffic throughput, and encrypted VPN traffic throughput, by nearly an
order-of-magnitude- particularly for small packets flowing in long duration connections.

Reference:
https://downloads.checkpoint.com/fileserver/SOURCE/direct/ID/10001/FILE/SecureXL_and_Nokia_IPSO_White_
Paper_20080401.pdf

QUESTION 53

Which command gives us a perspective of the number of kernel tables?

A. fw tab -t
B. fw tab -s
C. fw tab -n
D. fw tab -k

QUESTION 54

When Dynamic Dispatcher is enabled, connections are assigned dynamically with the exception of:

A. Threat Emulation
B. HTTPS
C. QOS
D. VoIP

QUESTION 55

SandBlast offers flexibility in implementation based on their individual business needs. What is an option for deployment of Check Point SandBlast Zero-Day Protection?

A. Smart Cloud Services
B. Load Sharing Mode Services
C. Threat Agent Solution
D. Public Cloud Services

QUESTION 56

Which of the following is NOT a component of Check Point Capsule?

A. Capsule Docs
B. Capsule Cloud
C. Capsule Enterprise
D. Capsule Workspace

QUESTION 57

What is the purpose of Priority Delta in VRRP?

A. When a box up, Effective Priority = Priority + Priority Delta
B. When an Interface is up, Effective Priority = Priority + Priority Delta
C. When an Interface fail, Effective Priority = Priority – Priority Delta
D. When a box fail, Effective Priority = Priority – Priority Delta

Explanation:
Each instance of VRRP running on a supported interface may monitor the link state of other interfaces. The monitored interfaces do not have to be running VRRP.
If a monitored interface loses its link state, then VRRP will decrement its priority over a VRID by the specified delta value and then will send out a new VRRP HELLO packet. If the new effective priority is less than the priority a backup platform has, then the backup platform will beging to send out its own HELLO packet.
Once the master sees this packet with a priority greater than its own, then it releases the VIP.

Reference:
https://supportcenter.checkpoint.com/supportcenter/portal?eventSubmit_doGoviewsolutiondetails=&solutionid=sk38524

QUESTION 58
What is the name of the secure application for Mail/Calendar for mobile devices?

A. Capsule Workspace
B. Capsule Mail
C. Capsule VPN
D. Secure Workspace

Reference:

https://www.checkpoint.com/products/mobile-secure-workspace/

QUESTION 59
Where do you create and modify the Mobile Access policy in R80?

A. SmartConsole
B. SmartMonitor
C. SmartEndpoint
D. SmartDashboard

QUESTION 60
SmartConsole R80 requires the following ports to be open for SmartEvent R80 management:

A. 19090,22
B. 19190,22
C. 18190,80
D. 19009,443

QUESTION 61
Which configuration file contains the structure of the Security Server showing the port numbers, corresponding protocol name, and status?

A. $FWDIR/database/fwauthd.conf
B. $FWDIR/conf/fwauth.conf
C. $FWDIR/conf/fwauthd.conf
D. $FWDIR/state/fwauthd.conf

QUESTION 62
What API command below creates a new host with the name "New Host" and IP address of "192.168.0.10"?

A. new host name "New Host" ip-address "192.168.0.10"
B. set host name "New Host" ip-address "192.168.0.10"
C. create host name "New Host" ip-address "192.168.0.10"
D. add host name "New Host" ip-address "192.168.0.10"

QUESTION 63
As a valid Mobile Access Method, what feature provides Capsule Connect/VPN?

A. That is used to deploy the mobile device as a generator of one-time passwords for authenticating to an RSA Authentication Manager.
B. Fill Layer4 VPN –SSL VPN that gives users network access to all mobile applications.
C. Full Layer3 VPN –IPSec VPN that gives users network access to all mobile applications.
D. You can make sure that documents are sent to the intended recipients only.

Reference:
https://sc1.checkpoint.com/documents/R77/CP_R77_Mobile_Access_WebAdmin/82201.htm

QUESTION 64
You find one of your cluster gateways showing "Down" when you run the "cphaprob stat" command. You then run the "clusterXL_admin up" on the down member but unfortunately the member continues to show down. What command do you run to determine the cause?

A. cphaprob –f register
B. cphaprob –d –s report
C. cpstat –f all
D. cphaprob –a list

QUESTION 65
In SmartEvent, what are the different types of automatic reactions that the administrator can configure?

A. Mail, Block Source, Block Event Activity, External Script, SNMP Trap
B. Mail, Block Source, Block Destination, Block Services, SNMP Trap
C. Mail, Block Source, Block Destination, External Script, SNMP Trap
D. Mail, Block Source, Block Event Activity, Packet Capture, SNMP Trap

Reference: https://sc1.checkpoint.com/documents/R76/CP_R76_SmartEvent_AdminGuide/17401.htm

QUESTION 66

Using mgmt_cli, what is the correct syntax to import a host object called Server_1 from the CLI?

A. mgmt_cli add-host "Server_1" ip_address "10.15.123.10" --format txt
B. mgmt_cli add host name "Server_1" ip-address "10.15.123.10" --format json
C. mgmt_cli add object-host "Server_1" ip-address "10.15.123.10" --format json
D. mgmt._cli add object "Server-1" ip-address "10.15.123.10" --format json

Example:

mgmt_cli add host name "New Host 1" ip-address "192.0.2.1" --format json
• "--format json" is optional. By default the output is presented in plain text.

Reference:
https://sc1.checkpoint.com/documents/latest/APIs/index.html#cli/add-host~v1.1%20

QUESTION 67

What are the steps to configure the HTTPS Inspection Policy?

A. Go to Manage&Settings > Blades > HTTPS Inspection > Configure in SmartDashboard
B. Go to Application&url filtering blade > Advanced > Https Inspection > Policy
C. Go to Manage&Settings > Blades > HTTPS Inspection > Policy
D. Go to Application&url filtering blade > Https Inspection > Policy

QUESTION 68

You want to store the GAIA configuration in a file for later reference. What command should you use?

A. write mem <filename>
B. show config –f <filename>
C. save config –o <filename>
D. save configuration <filename>

QUESTION 69

How do Capsule Connect and Capsule Workspace differ?

A. Capsule Connect provides a Layer3 VPN. Capsule Workspace provides a Desktop with usable applications.
B. Capsule Workspace can provide access to any application.
C. Capsule Connect provides Business data isolation.
D. Capsule Connect does not require an installed application at client.

QUESTION 70

You have existing dbedit scripts from R77. Can you use them with R80.10?

A. dbedit is not supported in R80.10
B. dbedit is fully supported in R80.10
C. You can use dbedit to modify threat prevention or access policies, but not create or modify layers
D. dbedit scripts are being replaced by mgmt_cli in R80.10

Reference:
https://www.checkpoint.com/downloads/product-related/r80.10-mgmt-architecture-overview.pdf

QUESTION 71

What is the command to see cluster status in cli expert mode?

A. fw ctl stat
B. clusterXL stat
C. clusterXL status
D. cphaprob stat

QUESTION 72

Which command is used to display status information for various components?

A. show all systems
B. show system messages
C. sysmess all
D. show sysenv all

Reference:

https://sc1.checkpoint.com/documents/R77/CP_R77_Gaia_AdminWebAdminGuide/html_frameset.htm?topic=doc
uments/R77/ CP_R77_Gaia_AdminWebAdminGuide/120709

QUESTION 73

What are the blades of Threat Prevention?

A. IPS, DLP, AntiVirus, AntiBot, Sandblast Threat Emulation/Extraction
B. DLP, AntiVirus, QoS, AntiBot, Sandblast Threat Emulation/Extraction
C. IPS, AntiVirus, AntiBot
D. IPS, AntiVirus, AntiBot, Sandblast Threat Emulation/Extraction

Reference:

 https://www.checkpoint.com/products/next-generation-threat-prevention/

QUESTION 74

For Management High Availability, which of the following is NOT a valid synchronization status?

A. Collision
B. Down
C. Lagging
D. Never been synchronized

Reference:

https://sc1.checkpoint.com/documents/R76/CP_R76_SecMan_WebAdmin/html_frameset.htm?topic=documents/
R76/ CP_R76_SecMan_WebAdmin/13132

QUESTION 75

Which process is available on any management product and on products that require direct GUI access, such as SmartEvent and provides GUI client communications, database manipulation, policy compilation and Management HA synchronization?

A. cpwd
B. fwd
C. cpd
D. fwm

Explanation:

Firewall Management (fwm) is available on any management product, including Multi-Domain and on products that requite direct GUI access, such as SmartEvent, It provides the following:
– GUI Client communication
– Database manipulation
– Policy Compilation
– Management HA sync

QUESTION 76

Under which file is the proxy arp configuration stored?

A. $FWDIR/state/proxy_arp.conf on the management server
B. $FWDIR/conf/local.arp on the management server
C. $FWDIR/state/_tmp/proxy.arp on the security gateway
D. $FWDIR/conf/local.arp on the gateway

QUESTION 77
What information is NOT collected from a Security Gateway in a CPINFO?

A. Firewall logs
B. Configuration and database files
C. System message logs
D. OS and network statistics

Reference:
https://supportcenter.checkpoint.com/supportcenter/portal?eventSubmit_doGoviewsolutiondetails=&solutionid=sk
92739

QUESTION 78

SandBlast appliances can be deployed in the following modes:

A. using a SPAN port to receive a copy of the traffic only
B. detect only
C. inline/prevent or detect
D. as a Mail Transfer Agent and as part of the traffic flow only

QUESTION 79

Traffic from source 192.168.1.1 is going to www.google.com. The Application Control Blade on the gateway is inspecting the traffic. Assuming acceleration is enabled which path is handling the traffic?

A. Slow Path
B. Medium Path
C. Fast Path
D. Accelerated Path

QUESTION 80

What is the difference between SSL VPN and IPSec VPN?

A. IPSec VPN does not require installation of a residient VPN client.
B. SSL VPN requires installation of a resident VPN client.
C. SSL VPN and IPSec VPN are the same.
D. IPSec VPN requires installation of a resident VPN client and SSL VPN requires only an installed Browser.

QUESTION 81

Which of the following will NOT affect acceleration?

A. Connections destined to or originated from the Security gateway
B. A 5-tuple match
C. Multicast packets
D. Connections that have a Handler (ICMP, FTP, H.323, etc.)

QUESTION 82

Which of the following is NOT a type of Check Point API available in R80.10?

A. Identity Awareness Web Services
B. OPSEC SDK
C. Mobile Access
D. Management

QUESTION 83

When an encrypted packet is decrypted, where does this happen?

A. Security policy
B. Inbound chain
C. Outbound chain
D. Decryption is not supported

QUESTION 84

John is using Management HA. Which Smartcenter should be connected to for making changes?

A. secondary Smartcenter
B. active Smartenter
C. connect virtual IP of Smartcenter HA
D. primary Smartcenter

QUESTION 85

What scenario indicates that SecureXL is enabled?

A. Dynamic objects are available in the Object Explorer
B. SecureXL can be disabled in cpconfig
C. fwaccel commands can be used in clish
D. Only one packet in a stream is seen in a fw monitor packet capture

QUESTION 86

What processes does CPM control?

A. Object-Store, Database changes, CPM Process and web-services
B. web-services, CPMI process, DLEserver, CPM process
C. DLEServer, Object-Store, CP Process and database changes
D. web_services, dle_server and object_Store

QUESTION 87

Which encryption algorithm is the least secured?

A. AES-128
B. AES-256
C. DES
D. 3DES

QUESTION 88

What is the command to check the status of the SmartEvent Correlation Unit?

A. fw ctl get int cpsead_stat
B. cpstat cpsead
C. fw ctl stat cpsemd
D. cp_conf get_stat cpsemd

Reference:

https://supportcenter.checkpoint.com/supportcenter/portal?eventSubmit_doGoviewsolutiondetails=&solutionid=sk113265

QUESTION 89

VPN Link Selection will perform the following when the primary VPN link goes down?

A. The Firewall will drop the packets.
B. The Firewall can update the Link Selection entries to start using a different link for the same tunnel.
C. The Firewall will send out the packet on all interfaces.
D. The Firewall will inform the client that the tunnel is down.

QUESTION 90

Which GUI client is supported in R80?

A. SmartProvisioning
B. SmartView Tracker
C. SmartView Monitor
D. SmartLog

QUESTION 91

Which command shows the current connections distributed by CoreXL FW instances?

A. fw ctl multik stat
B. fw ctl affinity -l
C. fw ctl instances -v
D. fw ctl iflist

QUESTION 92

How often does Threat Emulation download packages by default?

A. Once a week
B. Once an hour
C. Twice per day
D. Once per day

Reference:

https://sc1.checkpoint.com/documents/R77/CP_R77_ThreatPrevention_WebAdmin/101703.htm

QUESTION 93

You are investigating issues with to gateway cluster members are not able to establish the first initial cluster synchronization. What service is used by the FWD daemon to do a Full Synchronization?

A. TCP port 443
B. TCP port 257
C. TCP port 256
D. UDP port 8116

QUESTION 94

Which statement is true about ClusterXL?

A. Supports Dynamic Routing (Unicast and Multicast)
B. Supports Dynamic Routing (Unicast Only)
C. Supports Dynamic Routing (Multicast Only)
D. Does not support Dynamic Routing

Reference:

https://sc1.checkpoint.com/documents/R76/CP_R76_ClusterXL_AdminGuide/7300.htm

QUESTION 95

Which Check Point software blades could be enforced under Threat Prevention profile using Check Point R80.10 SmartConsole application?

A. IPS, Anti-Bot, URL Filtering, Application Control, Threat Emulation.
B. Firewall, IPS, Threat Emulation, Application Control.
C. IPS, Anti-Bot, Anti-Virus, Threat Emulation, Threat Extraction.
D. Firewall, IPS, Anti-Bot, Anti-Virus, Threat Emulation.

QUESTION 96

When gathering information about a gateway using CPINFO, what information is included or excluded when using the "-x" parameter?

A. Includes the registry
B. Gets information about the specified Virtual System
C. Does not resolve network addresses
D. Output excludes connection table

Reference:

https://www.networksecurityplus.net/2015/02/check-point-how-to-collect-cpinfo-cli.html

QUESTION 97

What component of R80 Management is used for indexing?

A. DBSync
B. API Server
C. fwm
D. SOLR

Reference:

https://www.checkpoint.com/downloads/product-related/r80.10-mgmt-architecture-overview.pdf

QUESTION 98

After making modifications to the $CVPNDIR/conf/cvpnd.C file, how would you restart the daemon?

A. cvpnd_restart
B. cvpnd_restart
C. cvpnd restart
D. cvpnrestart

QUESTION 99

What is the benefit of "tw monitor" over "tcpdump"?

A. "fw monitor" reveals Layer 2 information, while "tcpdump" acts at Layer 3.
B. "fw monitor" is also available for 64-Bit operating systems.
C. With "fw monitor", you can see the inspection points, which cannot be seen in "tcpdump"
D. "fw monitor" can be used from the CLI of the Management Server to collect information from multiple gateways.

QUESTION 100

What command can you use to have cpinfo display all installed hotfixes?

A. cpinfo -hf
B. cpinfo –y all
C. cpinfo –get hf
D. cpinfo installed_jumbo

QUESTION 101

What is considered Hybrid Emulation Mode?

A. Manual configuration of file types on emulation location.
B. Load sharing of emulation between an on premise appliance and the cloud.
C. Load sharing between OS behavior and CPU Level emulation.
D. High availability between the local SandBlast appliance and the cloud.

QUESTION 102

When setting up an externally managed log server, what is one item that will not be configured on the R80
Security Management Server?

A. IP
B. SIC
C. NAT
D. FQDN

QUESTION 103

Customer's R80 management server needs to be upgraded to R80.10. What is the best upgrade method when
the management server is not connected to the Internet?

A. Export R80 configuration, clean install R80.10 and import the configuration
B. CPUSE offline upgrade
C. CPUSE online upgrade
D. SmartUpdate upgrade

QUESTION 104

Which one of the following is true about Threat Emulation?

A. Takes less than a second to complete
B. Works on MS Office and PDF files only
C. Always delivers a file
D. Takes minutes to complete (less than 3 minutes)

QUESTION 105

What is the purpose of a SmartEvent Correlation Unit?

A. The SmartEvent Correlation Unit is designed to check the connection reliability from SmartConsole to the SmartEvent Server.
B. The SmartEvent Correlation Unit's task it to assign severity levels to the identified events.
C. The Correlation unit role is to evaluate logs from the log server component to identify patterns/threats and convert them to events.
D. The SmartEvent Correlation Unit is designed to check the availability of the SmartReporter Server.

QUESTION 106

What is a best practice before starting to troubleshoot using the "fw monitor" tool?

A. Run the command: fw monitor debug on
B. Clear the connections table
C. Disable CoreXL
D. Disable SecureXL

QUESTION 107

SmartEvent does NOT use which of the following procedures to identify events:

A. Matching a log against each event definition
B. Create an event candidate
C. Matching a log against local exclusions
D. Matching a log against global exclusions

Explanation:

Events are detected by the SmartEvent Correlation Unit. The Correlation Unit task is to scan logs for criteria that match an Event Definition. SmartEvent uses these procedures to identify events:
• Matching a Log Against Global Exclusions
• Matching a Log Against Each Event Definition
• Creating an Event Candidate
• When a Candidate Becomes an Event

Reference:

 https://sc1.checkpoint.com/documents/R76/CP_R76_SmartEvent_AdminGuide/17401.htm

QUESTION 108

What is the most recommended way to install patches and hotfixes?

A. CPUSE Check Point Update Service Engine
B. rpm -Uv
C. Software Update Service
D. UnixinstallScript

QUESTION 109

Which web services protocol is used to communicate to the Check Point R80 Identity Awareness Web API?

A. SOAP
B. REST
C. XLANG
D. XML-RPC

Explanation:

The Identity Web API uses the REST protocol over SSL. The requests and responses are HTTP and in JSON format.

Reference:

https://sc1.checkpoint.com/documents/R80.10/WebAdminGuides/EN/CP_R80.10_IdentityAwareness_AdminGuide/html_frameset.htm?
topic=documents/R80.10/WebAdminGuides/EN/CP_R80.10_IdentityAwareness_AdminGuide/148699

QUESTION 110

What is mandatory for ClusterXL to work properly?

A. The number of cores must be the same on every participating cluster node
B. The Magic MAC number must be unique per cluster node
C. The Sync interface must not have an IP address configured
D. If you have "Non-monitored Private" interfaces, the number of those interfaces must be the same on all cluster members

QUESTION 111

Please choose correct command to add an "emailserver1" host with IP address 10.50.23.90 using GAiA management CLI?

A. host name myHost12 ip-address 10.50.23.90
B. mgmt: add host name ip-address 10.50.23.90
C. add host name emailserver1 ip-address 10.50.23.90
D. mgmt: add host name emailserver1 ip-address 10.50.23.90

QUESTION 112

Using Threat Emulation technologies, what is the best way to block .exe and .bat file types?

A. enable DLP and select.exe and .bat file type
B. enable .exe & .bat protection in IPS Policy
C. create FW rule for particular protocol
D. tecli advanced attributes set prohibited_file_types exe.bat

QUESTION 113

What is the recommended number of physical network interfaces in a Mobile Access cluster deployment?

A. 4 Interfaces – an interface leading to the organization, a second interface leading to the internet, a third interface for synchronization, a fourth interface leading to the Security Management Server.
B. 3 Interfaces – an interface leading to the organization, a second interface leading to the Internet, a third interface for synchronization.
C. 1 Interface – an interface leading to the organization and the Internet, and configure for synchronization.
D. 2 Interfaces – a data interface leading to the organization and the Internet, a second interface for synchronization.

Reference:

https://sc1.checkpoint.com/documents/R76/CP_R76_Mobile_Access_WebAdmin/41723.htm

QUESTION 114

Which process handles connection from SmartConsole R80?

A. fwd
B. cpmd
C. cpm
D. cpd

QUESTION 115

What will SmartEvent automatically define as events?

A. Firewall
B. VPN
C. IPS
D. HTTPS

Reference:

https://sc1.checkpoint.com/documents/R80/CP_R80_LoggingAndMonitoring/html_frameset.htm?topic=documents/R80/_CP_R80_LoggingAndMonitoring/131915

QUESTION 116

With MTA (Mail Transfer Agent) enabled the gateways manages SMTP traffic and holds external email with potentially malicious attachments. What is required in order to enable MTA (Mail Transfer Agent) functionality in the Security Gateway?

A. Threat Cloud Intelligence
B. Threat Prevention Software Blade Package
C. Endpoint Total Protection
D. Traffic on port 25

QUESTION 117

What is not a purpose of the deployment of Check Point API?

A. Execute an automated script to perform common tasks
B. Create a customized GUI Client for manipulating the objects database
C. Create products that use and enhance the Check Point solution
D. Integrate Check Point products with 3rd party solution

Reference:

Check Point APIs Reference Guide R80 PDF

QUESTION 118

You need to change the number of firewall Instances used by CoreXL. How can you achieve this goal?

A. edit fwaffinity.conf; reboot required
B. cpconfig; reboot required
C. edit fwaffinity.conf; reboot not required
D. cpconfig; reboot not required

Reference:

https://sc1.checkpoint.com/documents/R76/CP_R76_PerformanceTuning_WebAdmin/6731.htm#o94530

QUESTION 119

Fill in the blank: Identity Awareness AD-Query is using the Microsoft_________________API to learn users from AD.

A. WMI
B. Eventvwr
C. XML
D. Services.msc

Reference:

http://dl3.checkpoint.com/paid/e0/e01d7daa665096a4941f930f2567d29e/CP_R80.10_IdentityAwareness_Admin Guide.pdf? HashKey=1553448919_104b8593c2a2087ec2ffe8e86b314d66&xtn=.pdf

QUESTION 120
The essential means by which state synchronization works to provide failover in the event an active member goes down,_________________

A. ccp
B. cphaconf
C. cphad
D. cphastart

Reference: https://etherealmind.com/checkpoint-nokia-firewall-cluster-xl/?doing_wp_cron=1553442264.8447830677032470703125

QUESTION 121

Which statement is most correct regarding about "CoreXL Dynamic Dispatcher"?

A. The CoreXL FW instances assignment mechanism is based on Source MAC addresses, Destination MAC addresses
B. The CoreXL FW instances assignment mechanism is based on the utilization of CPU cores
C. The CoreXL FW instances assignment mechanism is based on IP Protocol type
D. The CoreXL FW instances assignment mechanism is based on Source IP addresses, Destination IP addresses, and the IP 'Protocol' type

Reference:

https://supportcenter.checkpoint.com/supportcenter/portal?eventSubmit_doGoviewsolutiondetails=&solutionid=sk105261

QUESTION 122

Pamela is Cyber Security Engineer working for Global Instance Firm with large scale deployment of Check Point Enterprise Appliances using GAiA/R80.10. Company's Developer Team is having random access issue to newly deployed Application Server in DMZ's Application Server Farm Tier and blames DMZ Security Gateway as root cause. The ticket has been created and issue is at Pamela's desk for an investigation. Pamela decides to use Check Point's Packet Analyzer Tool- fw monitor to iron out the issue during approved Maintenance window.

What do you recommend as the best suggestion for Pamela to make sure she successfully captures entire traffic in context of Firewall and problematic traffic?

A. Pamela should check SecureXL status on DMZ Security gateway and if it's turned ON. She should turn OFF SecureXL before using fw monitor to avoid misleading traffic captures.
B. Pamela should check SecureXL status on DMZ Security Gateway and if it's turned OFF. She should turn ON SecureXL before using fw monitor to avoid misleading traffic captures.
C. Pamela should use tcpdump over fw monitor tool as tcpdump works at OS-level and captures entire traffic.
D. Pamela should use snoop over fw monitor tool as snoop works at NIC driver level and captures entire traffic.

QUESTION 123

Fill in the blank: The "fw monitor" tool can be best used to troubleshoot_______________________.

A. AV issues
B. VPN errors
C. Network issues
D. Authentication issues

QUESTION 124

In which formats can Threat Emulation forensics reports be viewed in?

A. TXT, XML and CSV
B. PDF and TXT
C. PDF, HTML, and XML
D. PDF and HTML

QUESTION 125

What kind of information would you expect to see using the sim affinity command?

A. The VMACs used in a Security Gateway cluster
B. The involved firewall kernel modules in inbound and outbound packet chain
C. Overview over SecureXL templated connections
D. Network interfaces and core distribution used for CoreXL

QUESTION 126

What cloud-based SandBlast Mobile application is used to register new devices and users?

A. Check Point Protect Application
B. Management Dashboard
C. Behavior Risk Engine
D. Check Point Gateway

QUESTION 127

In the Firewall chain mode FFF refers to:

A. Stateful Packets
B. No Match
C. All Packets
D. Stateless Packets

Reference:

http://dkcheckpoint.blogspot.com/2016/07/chapter-2-chain-module.html

QUESTION 128

Which of the following commands shows the status of processes?

A. cpwd_admin -l
B. cpwd -l
C. cpwd admin_list
D. cpwd_admin list

Reference:

https://community.checkpoint.com/thread/8054-cpwdadmin-list-overview-sms

QUESTION 129

What is the valid range for VRID value in VRRP configuration?

A. 1 - 254
B. 1 - 255
C. 0 - 254
D. 0 - 255

Explanation:

Virtual Router ID - Enter a unique ID number for this virtual router. The range of valid values is 1 to 255.

Reference:

 https://sc1.checkpoint.com/documents/R76/CP_R76_Gaia_WebAdmin/87911.htm

QUESTION 130

To ensure that VMAC mode is enabled, which CLI command should you run on all cluster members?

A. fw ctl set int fwha vmac global param enabled
B. fw ctl get int vmac global param enabled; result of command should return value 1
C. cphaprob-a if
D. fw ctl get int fwha_vmac_global_param_enabled; result of command should return value 1

Reference:

https://sc1.checkpoint.com/documents/R76/CP_R76_ClusterXL_AdminGuide/7292.htm

QUESTION 131

For best practices, what is the recommended time for automatic unlocking of locked admin accounts?

A. 20 minutes

B. 15 minutes
C. Admin account cannot be unlocked automatically
D. 30 minutes at least

QUESTION 132

When SecureXL is enabled, all packets should be accelerated, except packets that match the following conditions:

A. All UDP packets
B. All IPv6 Traffic
C. All packets that match a rule whose source or destination is the Outside Corporate Network
D. CIFS packets

QUESTION 133

On what port does the CPM process run?

A. TCP 857
B. TCP 18192
C. TCP 900
D. TCP 19009

Reference:

https://sc1.checkpoint.com/documents/R80/CP_R80_MultiDomainSecurity/html_frameset.htm?topic=documents/
R80/_CP_R80_MultiDomainSecurity/15420

QUESTION 134

What is the SandBlast Agent designed to do?

A. Performs OS-level sandboxing for SandBlast Cloud architecture
B. Ensure the Check Point SandBlast services is running on the end user's system
C. If malware enters an end user's system, the SandBlast Agent prevents the malware from spreading with the network
D. Clean up email sent with malicious attachments

Reference:

https://www.checkpoint.com/downloads/product-related/datasheets/ds-sandblast-agent.pdf

QUESTION 135

What is correct statement about Security Gateway and Security Management Server failover in Check Point R80.X in terms of Check Point Redundancy driven solution?

A. Security Gateway failover is an automatic procedure but Security Management Server failover is a manual procedure.
B. Security Gateway failover as well as Security Management Server failover is a manual procedure.
C. Security Gateway failover is a manual procedure but Security Management Server failover is an automatic procedure.
D. Security Gateway failover as well as Security Management Server failover is an automatic procedure.

QUESTION 136

SandBlast agent extends 0 day prevention to what part of the network?

A. Web Browsers and user devices
B. DMZ server
C. Cloud
D. Email servers

QUESTION 137

In Logging and Monitoring, the tracking options are Log, Detailed Log and Extended Log. Which of the following options can you add to each Log, Detailed Log and Extended Log?

A. Accounting
B. Suppression
C. Accounting/Suppression
D. Accounting/Extended

Reference:

https://sc1.checkpoint.com/documents/R80/CP_R80_LoggingAndMonitoring/html_frameset.htm?topic=documents/R80/ CP_R80_LoggingAndMonitoring/131914

QUESTION 138

Which file contains the host address to be published, the MAC address that needs to be associated with the IP Address, and the unique IP of the interface that responds to ARP request?

A. /opt/CPshrd-R80/conf/local.arp
B. /var/opt/CPshrd-R80/conf/local.arp
C. $CPDIR/conf/local.arp
D. $FWDIR/conf/local.arp

QUESTION 139

With SecureXL enabled, accelerated packets will pass through the following:

A. Network Interface Card, OSI Network Layer, OS IP Stack, and the Acceleration Device
B. Network Interface Card, Check Point Firewall Kernal, and the Acceleration Device
C. Network Interface Card and the Acceleration Device
D. Network Interface Card, OSI Network Layer, and the Acceleration Device

QUESTION 140

You notice that your firewall is under a DDoS attack and would like to enable the Penalty Box feature, which command you use?

A. sim erdos –e 1
B. sim erdos – m 1
C. sim erdos –v 1
D. sim erdos –x 1

QUESTION 141

During the Check Point Stateful Inspection Process, for packets that do not pass Firewall Kernel Inspection and are rejected by the rule definition, packets are:

A. Dropped without sending a negative acknowledgment
B. Dropped without logs and without sending a negative acknowledgment
C. Dropped with negative acknowledgment
D. Dropped with logs and without sending a negative acknowledgment

QUESTION 142

Vanessa is firewall administrator in her company. Her company is using Check Point firewall on a central and several remote locations which are managed centrally by R77.30 Security Management Server. On central location is installed R77.30 Gateway on Open server. Remote locations are using Check Point UTM-1570 series appliances with R75.30 and some of them are using a UTM-1-Edge-X or Edge-W with latest available firmware. She is in process of migrating to R80.

What can cause Vanessa unnecessary problems, if she didn't check all requirements for migration to R80?

A. Missing an installed R77.20 Add-on on Security Management Server
B. Unsupported firmware on UTM-1 Edge-W appliance
C. Unsupported version on UTM-1 570 series appliance
D. Unsupported appliances on remote locations

QUESTION 143

Please choose the path to monitor the compliance status of the Check Point R80.10 based management.

A. Gateways & Servers --> Compliance View
B. Compliance blade not available under R80.10
C. Logs & Monitor --> New Tab --> Open compliance View
D. Security & Policies --> New Tab --> Compliance View

QUESTION 144

When using CPSTAT, what is the default port used by the AMON server?

A. 18191
B. 18192
C. 18194
D. 18190

Reference:

https://sc1.checkpoint.com/documents/R80.20_M1/WebAdminGuides/EN/CP_R80.20_M1_CLI_ReferenceGuide/html_frameset.htm?topic=documents/
R80.20_M1/WebAdminGuides/EN/CP_R80.20_M1_CLI_ReferenceGuide/162534

QUESTION 145

What must you do first if "fwm sic_reset" could not be completed?

A. Cpstop then find keyword "certificate" in objects_5_0.C and delete the section
B. Reinitialize SIC on the security gateway then run "fw unloadlocal"
C. Reset SIC from Smart Dashboard
D. Change internal CA via cpconfig

QUESTION 146

Check Point security components are divided into the following components:

A. GUI Client, Security Gateway, WebUI Interface
B. GUI Client, Security Management, Security Gateway
C. Security Gateway, WebUI Interface, Consolidated Security Logs
D. Security Management, Security Gateway, Consolidate Security Logs

QUESTION 147

You have a Geo-Protection policy blocking Australia and a number of other countries. Your network now requires a Check Point Firewall to be installed in Sydney, Australia.

What must you do to get SIC to work?

A. Remove Geo-Protection, as the IP-to-country database is updated externally, and you have no control of this.
B. Create a rule at the top in the Sydney firewall to allow control traffic from your network
C. Nothing - Check Point control connections function regardless of Geo-Protection policy
D. Create a rule at the top in your Check Point firewall to bypass the Geo-Protection

Reference:

https://sc1.checkpoint.com/documents/R76/CP_R76_Firewall_WebAdmin/92707.htm

QUESTION 148

In the Check Point Firewall Kernel Module, each Kernel is associated with a key, which specifies the type of traffic applicable to the chain module. For Stateful Mode configuration, chain modules marked with____will not apply.

A. ffff
B. 1
C. 3
D. 2

Reference:

http://dkcheckpoint.blogspot.com/2016/07/chapter-2-chain-module.html

QUESTION 149

In what way is Secure Network Distributor (SND) a relevant feature of the Security Gateway?

A. SND is a feature to accelerate multiple SSL VPN connections
B. SND is an alternative to IPSec Main Mode, using only 3 packets
C. SND is used to distribute packets among Firewall instances
D. SND is a feature of fw monitor to capture accelerated packets

QUESTION 150

Which NAT rules are prioritized first?

A. Post-Automatic/Manual NAT rules
B. Manual/Pre-Automatic NAT
C. Automatic Hide NAT
D. Automatic Static NAT

QUESTION 151

What is the most ideal Synchronization Status for Security Management Server High Availability deployment?

A. Lagging
B. Synchronized
C. Never been synchronized
D. Collision

QUESTION 152

You can access the ThreatCloud Repository from:

A. R80.10 SmartConsole and Application Wiki
B. Threat Prevention and Threat Tools
C. Threat Wiki and Check Point Website
D. R80.10 SmartConsole and Threat Prevention

Reference:

https://sc1.checkpoint.com/documents/R80.10/WebAdminGuides/EN/CP_R80.10_ThreatPrevention_AdminGuide/html_frameset.htm?topic=documents/
R80.10/WebAdminGuides/EN/CP_R80.10_ThreatPrevention_AdminGuide/131285

QUESTION 153
Which path below is available only when CoreXL is enabled?

A. Slow path
B. Firewall path
C. Medium path
D. Accelerated path

QUESTION 154

You want to verify if your management server is ready to upgrade to R80.10. What tool could you use in this

process?

A. migrate export
B. upgrade_tools verify
C. pre_upgrade_verifier
D. migrate import

QUESTION 155

GAiA Software update packages can be imported and installed offline in situation where:

A. Security Gateway with GAiA does NOT have SFTP access to Internet
B. Security Gateway with GAiA does NOT have access to Internet.
C. Security Gateway with GAiA does NOT have SSH access to Internet.
D. The desired CPUSE package is ONLY available in the Check Point CLOUD.

QUESTION 156

Which of the following technologies extracts detailed information from packets and stores that information in state
tables?

A. INSPECT Engine
B. Stateful Inspection
C. Packet Filtering
D. Application Layer Firewall

Reference:

https://www.checkpoint.com/training/ccsa/chapter1/

QUESTION 157

Which tool provides a list of trusted files to the administrator so they can specify to the Threat Prevention blade
that these files do not need to be scanned or analyzed?

A. ThreatWiki
B. Whitelist Files
C. AppWiki
D. IPS Protections

Reference:

https://sc1.checkpoint.com/documents/R77/CP_R77_ThreatPrevention_WebAdmin/101703.htm

QUESTION 158

Which Check Point software blade provides Application Security and identity control?

A. Identity Awareness
B. Data Loss Prevention
C. URL Filtering
D. Application Control

QUESTION 159

Which of the following is **NOT** an alert option?

A. SNMP
B. High alert
C. Mail
D. User defined alert

Reference:

https://sc1.checkpoint.com/documents/R77/CP_R77_SmartViewMonitor_AdminGuide/101104.htm

QUESTION 160

What does it mean if Deyra sees the gateway status? (Choose the BEST answer.)

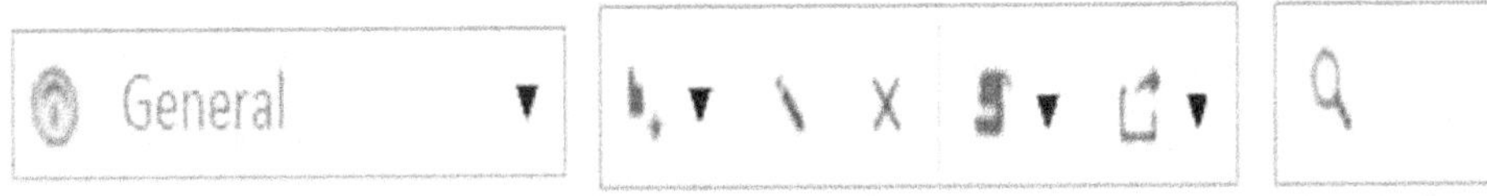

Status	Name	IP	Version	Active Blade
✕	A-GW	10.1.1.1	R80	
✓	SMS	10.1.1.101	R80	

A. SmartCenter Server cannot reach this Security Gateway.
B. There is a blade reporting a problem.
C. VPN software blade is reporting a malfunction.
D. Security Gateway's MGNT NIC card is disconnected.

Reference:

https://sc1.checkpoint.com/sc/SolutionsStatics/NEW_SK_NOID1493612962436/active1704302237.fw.png

QUESTION 161

Ken wants to obtain a configuration lock from other administrator on R80 Security Management Server. He can

do this via WebUI or via CLI. Which command should he use in CLI? (Choose the correct answer.)

A. `remove database lock`
B. The database feature has one command `lock database override`.
C. `override database lock`
D. The database feature has two commands lock database override and unlock database. Both will work.

Reference:

https://sc1.checkpoint.com/documents/R76/CP_R76_Gaia_WebAdmin/75697.htm#o73091

QUESTION 162

What will be the effect of running the following command on the Security Management Server?

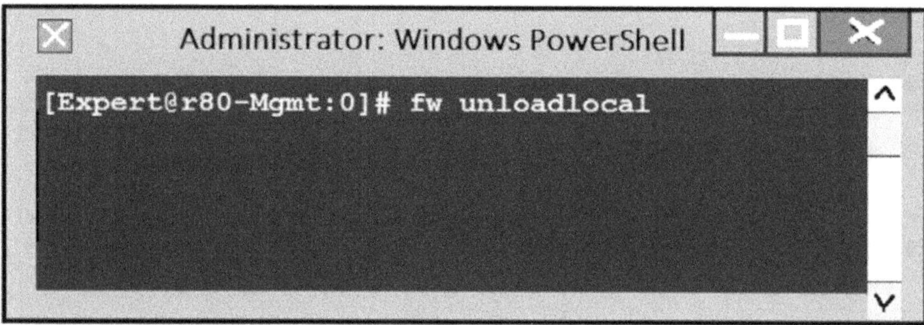

A. Remove the installed Security Policy.
B. Remove the local ACL lists.
C. No effect.
D. Reset SIC on all gateways.

Reference:

https://sc1.checkpoint.com/documents/R77/CP_R77_SecurityGatewayTech_WebAdmin/6751.htm

QUESTION 163

Which of the following is **NOT** a VPN routing option available in a star community?

A. To satellites through center only.
B. To center, or through the center to other satellites, to Internet and other VPN targets.
C. To center and to other satellites through center.
D. To center only.

Reference:

https://sc1.checkpoint.com/documents/R80/CP_R80BC_VPN/html_frameset.htm

QUESTION 164

Fill in the blank. Once a certificate is revoked from the Security Gateway by the Security Management Server, the certificate information is__________________________________

A. Sent to the Internal Certificate Authority.
B. Sent to the Security Administrator.
C. Stored on the Security Management Server.
D. Stored on the Certificate Revocation List.

QUESTION 165

After trust has been established between the Check Point components, what is TRUE about name and IP-address changes?

A. Security Gateway IP-address cannot be changed without re-establishing the trust.

B. The Security Gateway name cannot be changed in command line without re-establishing trust.
C. The Security Management Server name cannot be changed in SmartConsole without re-establishing trust.
D. The Security Management Server IP-address cannot be changed without re-establishing the trust.

QUESTION 166

Which Check Point feature enables application scanning and the detection?

A. Application Dictionary
B. AppWiki
C. Application Library
D. CPApp

Reference:

 https://www.checkpoint.com/products/application-control-software-blade/

QUESTION 167

Fill in the blank: The R80 SmartConsole, SmartEvent GUI client, and_________consolidate billions of logs and shows then as prioritized security events.

A. SmartMonitor
B. SmartView Web Application
C. SmartReporter
D. SmartTracker

Reference:

https://sc1.checkpoint.com/documents/R80/CP_R80_LoggingAndMonitoring/html_frameset.htm?topic=documents/R80/ CP_R80_LoggingAndMonitoring/131915

QUESTION 168

Office mode means that:
A. SecurID client assigns a routable MAC address. After the user authenticates for a tunnel, the VPN gateway assigns a routable IP address to the remote client.
B. Users authenticate with an Internet browser and use secure HTTPS connection.
C. Local ISP (Internet service Provider) assigns a non-routable IP address to the remote user.
D. Allows a security gateway to assign a remote client an IP address. After the user authenticates for a tunnel, the VPN gateway assigns a routable IP address to the remote client.

Reference:

https://supportcenter.checkpoint.com/supportcenter/portal?eventSubmit_doGoviewsolutiondetails=&solutionid=sk30545

QUESTION 169

When attempting to start a VPN tunnel, in the logs the error "no proposal chosen" is seen numerous times. No other VPN-related entries are present. Which phase of the VPN negotiations has failed?

A. IKE Phase 1
B. IPSEC Phase 2
C. IPSEC Phase 1
D. IKE Phase 2

QUESTION 170

Fill in the blank: Browser-based Authentication sends users to a web page to acquire identities using__________.
A. User Directory

B. Captive Portal and Transparent Kerberos Authentication
C. Captive Portal
D. UserCheck

Reference:

https://sc1.checkpoint.com/documents/R76/CP_R76_IdentityAwareness_AdminGuide/62050.htm

QUESTION 171

One of major features in R80 SmartConsole is concurrent administration.

Which of the following is NOT possible considering that AdminA, AdminB and AdminC are editing the same Security Policy?

A. A lock icon shows that a rule or an object is locked and will be available.
B. AdminA and AdminB are editing the same rule at the same time.
C. A lock icon next to a rule informs that any Administrator is working on this particular rule.
D. AdminA, AdminB and AdminC are editing three different rules at the same time.

Reference: http://downloads.checkpoint.com/dc/download.htm?ID=65846

QUESTION 172

After the initial installation on Check Point appliance, you notice that the Management-interface and default

gateway are incorrect. Which commands could you use to set the IP to 192.168.80.200/24 and default gateway to

192.168.80.1.

A. set interface Mgmt ipv4-address 192.168.80.200 mask-length 24 set static-route default nexthop gateway
   address 192.168.80.1 onsave config
B. set interface Mgmt ipv4-address 192.168.80.200 255.255.255.0add static-route 0.0.0.0. 0.0.0.0 gw
   192.168.80.1 on
   save config
C. set interface Mgmt ipv4-address 192.168.80.200 255.255.255.0set static-route 0.0.0.0. 0.0.0.0 gw
   192.168.80.1 on
   save config
D. set interface Mgmt ipv4-address 192.168.80.200 mask-length 24 add static-route default nexthop gateway
   address 192.168.80.1 onsave config

QUESTION 173

Tom has connected to the R80 Management Server remotely using SmartConsole and is in the process of
making some Rule Base changes, when he suddenly loses connectivity. Connectivity is restored shortly
afterward.

What will happen to the changes already made?

A. Tom's changes will have been stored on the Management when he reconnects and he will not lose any of his
   work.
B. Tom will have to reboot his SmartConsole computer, and access the Management cache store on that
   computer, which is only accessible after a reboot.
C. Tom's changes will be lost since he lost connectivity and he will have to start again.
D. Tom will have to reboot his SmartConsole computer, clear to cache, and restore changes.

QUESTION 174

What key is used to save the current CPView page in a filename format `cpview_"cpview process ID".cap"number of captures"`?

A. S
B. W
C. C
D. Space bar

Reference:

QUESTION 175

Joey want to configure NTP on R80 Security Management Server. He decided to do this via WebUI. What is the correct address to access the Web UI for Gaia platform via browser?

A. https://<Device_IP_Adress>
B. http://<Device IP_Address>:443
C. https://<Device_IP_Address>:10000
D. https://<Device_IP_Address>:4434

Reference:

https://sc1.checkpoint.com/documents/R77/CP_R77_Gaia_AdminWebAdminGuide/html_frameset.htm?topic=documents/R77/CP_R77_Gaia_AdminWebAdminGuide/75930

QUESTION 176

Fill in the blank: Permanent VPN tunnels can be set on all tunnels in the community, on all tunnels for specific gateways, or_____________________

A. On all satellite gateway to satellite gateway tunnels
B. On specific tunnels for specific gateways
C. On specific tunnels in the community
D. On specific satellite gateway to central gateway tunnels

Reference:

https://sc1.checkpoint.com/documents/R77/CP_R77_VPN_AdminGuide/html_frameset.htm?topic=documents/R77/CP_R77_VPN_AdminGuide/14018

QUESTION 177

True or False: In a Distributed Environment, a Central License can be installed via CLI on a Security Gateway.

A. True, CLI is the prefer method for Licensing
B. False, Central License are handled via Security Management Server
C. False, Central Licenses are installed via Gaia on Security Gateways
D. True, Central License can be installed with CPLIC command on a Security Gateway

QUESTION 178

Which of the following is an identity acquisition method that allows a Security Gateway to identify Active Directory users and computers?

A. UserCheck
B. Active Directory Query
C. Account Unit Query
D. User Directory Query

Reference :

https://sc1.checkpoint.com/documents/R76/CP_R76_IdentityAwareness_AdminGuide/62402.htm

QUESTION 179

Which command is used to add users to or from existing roles?

```
A. Add rba user <User Name> roles <List>
B. Add rba user <User Name>
C. Add user <User Name> roles <List>
D. Add user <User Name>
```

Reference:
https://sc1.checkpoint.com/documents/R76/CP_R76_Gaia_WebAdmin/73101.htm

QUESTION 180

Which option, when applied to a rule, allows traffic to VPN gateways in specific VPN communities?

A. All Connections (Clear or Encrypted)
B. Accept all encrypted traffic
C. Specific VPN Communities
D. All Site-to-Site VPN Communities

QUESTION 181

Which of the following blades is NOT subscription-based and therefore does not have to be renewed on a regular basis?

A. Application Control
B. Threat Emulation
C. Anti-Virus
D. Advanced Networking Blade

QUESTION 182

You have created a rule at the top of your Rule Base to permit Guest Wireless access to the Internet. However, when guest users attempt to reach the Internet, they are not seeing the splash page to accept your Terms of Service, and cannot access the Internet. How can you fix this?

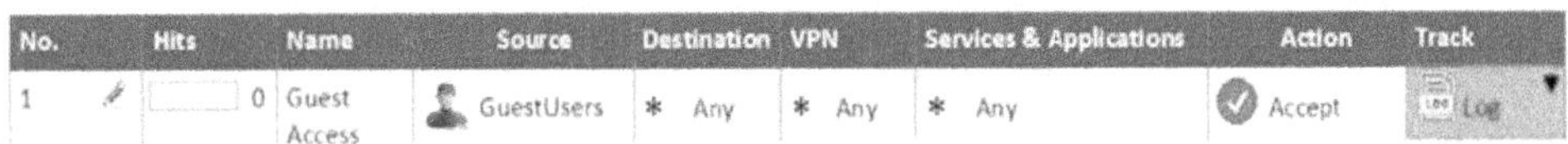

A. Right click Accept in the rule, select "More", and then check 'Enable Identity Captive Portal'.
B. On the firewall object, Legacy Authentication screen, check 'Enable Identity Captive Portal'.
C. In the Captive Portal screen of Global Properties, check 'Enable Identity Captive Portal'.
D. On the Security Management Server object, check the box 'Identity Logging'.

Reference:
https://sc1.checkpoint.com/documents/R80.20_GA/WebAdminGuides/EN/CP_R80.20_NextGenSecurityGateway_Guide/html_frameset.htm?
topic=documents/R80.20_GA/WebAdminGuides/EN/CP_R80.20_NextGenSecurityGateway_Guide/136978

QUESTION 183

Fill in the blank: A new license should be generated and installed in all of the following situations **EXCEPT** when

A. The license is attached to the wrong Security Gateway.
B. The existing license expires.
C. The license is upgraded.
D. The IP address of the Security Management or Security Gateway has changed.

QUESTION 184

If there are two administration logged in at the same time to the SmartConsole, and there are objects locked for editing, what must be done to make them available or other administrators? (Choose the BEST answer.)

A. Publish or discard the session.
B. Revert the session.
C. Save and install the Policy.
D. Delete older versions of database.

Reference:

https://sc1.checkpoint.com/documents/R80/CP_R80_SecMGMT/html_frameset.htm?topic=documents/R80/CP_R80_SecMGMT/126197

QUESTION 185

Fill in the blanks: A__________license requires an administrator to designate a gateway for attachment whereas a________________license is automatically attached to aSecurity Gateway.

A. Formal; corporate
B. Local; formal
C. Local; central
D. Central; local

Reference:

https://sc1.checkpoint.com/documents/R76/CP_R76_Installation_and_Upgrade_Guide-webAdmin/13128.htm

QUESTION 186

Fill in the blank: Authentication rules are defined for__________.

A. User groups
B. Users using UserCheck
C. Individual users
D. All users in the database

Reference:

https://sc1.checkpoint.com/documents/R76/CP_R76_SGW_WebAdmin/6721.htm

QUESTION 187

How is communication between different Check Point components secured in R80? As with all questions, select the BEST answer.

A. By using IPSEC
B. By using SIC
C. By using ICA
D. By using 3DES

Reference:

https://sc1.checkpoint.com/documents/R80/CP_R80_SecMGMT/html_frameset.htm?topic=documents/R80/CP_R80_SecMGMT/125443

QUESTION 188

Which feature is NOT provided by all Check Point Mobile Access solutions?

A. Support for IPv6
B. Granular access control
C. Strong user authentication
D. Secure connectivity

Explanation:

Types of Solutions
All of Check Point's Remote Access solutions provide: Enterprise-grade, secure connectivity to corporate
- resources.Strong user authentication.
- Granular access control.

QUESTION 189

Fill in the blank: A__________VPN deployment is used to provide remote users with secure access to internal corporate resources by authenticating the user through an internet browser.

A. Clientless remote access
B. Clientless direct access
C. Client-based remote access
D. Direct access

Reference:

https://sc1.checkpoint.com/documents/R80/CP_R80BC_Firewall/html_frameset.htm?topic=documents/R80/CP_R80BC_Firewall/92704

QUESTION 190

At what point is the Internal Certificate Authority (ICA) created?

A. Upon creation of a certificate.
B. During the primary Security Management Server installation process.
C. When an administrator decides to create one.
D. When an administrator initially logs into SmartConsole.

Reference:

https://sc1.checkpoint.com/documents/R76/CP_R76_SecMan_WebAdmin/html_frameset.htm?topic=documents/
R76/ CP_R76_SecMan_WebAdmin/13118

QUESTION 191

True or False: In R80, more than one administrator can login to the Security Management Server with write permission at the same time.

A. False, this feature has to be enabled in the Global Properties.
B. True, every administrator works in a session that is independent of the other administrators.
C. True, every administrator works on a different database that is independent of the other administrators.
D. False, only one administrator can login with write permission.

QUESTION 192

There are two R77.30 Security Gateways in the Firewall Cluster. They are named FW_A and FW_B. The cluster is configured to work as HA (High availability) with default cluster configuration. FW_A is configured to have higher priority than FW_B. FW_A was active and processing the traffic in the morning. FW_B was standby. Around 1100 am, its interfaces went down and this caused a failover. FW_B became active. After an hour, FW_A's interface issues were resolved and it became operational.

When it re-joins the cluster, will it become active automatically?

A. No, since 'maintain' current active cluster member' option on the cluster object properties is enabled by default.
B. No, since 'maintain' current active cluster member' option is enabled by default on the Global Properties.
C. Yes, since 'Switch to higher priority cluster member' option on the cluster object properties is enabled by default.
D. Yes, since 'Switch to higher priority cluster member' option is enabled by default on the Global Properties.

Reference:

http://dl3.checkpoint.com/paid/7e/7ef174cf00762ceaf228384ea20ea64a/CP_R77_ClusterXL_AdminGuide.pdf?
HashKey=1479822138_31410b1f8360074be87fd8f1ab682464&xtn=.pdf

QUESTION 193

Fill in the blank: The IPS policy for pre-R80 gateways is installed during the__________.

A. Firewall policy install
B. Threat Prevention policy install
C. Anti-bot policy install
D. Access Control policy install

QUESTION 194

How many users can have read/write access in Gaia at one time?

A. Infinite
B. One
C. Three
D. Two

QUESTION 195

Which software blade does **NOT** accompany the Threat Prevention policy?

A. Anti-virus
B. IPS
C. Threat Emulation
D. Application Control and URL Filtering

QUESTION 196

To optimize Rule Base efficiency, the most hit rules should be where?

A. Removed from the Rule Base.
B. Towards the middle of the Rule Base.
C. Towards the top of the Rule Base.
D. Towards the bottom of the Rule Base.

QUESTION 197

What is the default shell for the command line interface?

A. Expert
B. Clish
C. Admin
D. Normal

Explanation:

The default shell of the CLI is called clish
Reference: https://sc1.checkpoint.com/documents/R76/CP_R76_Gaia_WebAdmin/75697.htm

QUESTION 198
You plan to automate creating new objects using new R80 Management API. You decide to use GAIA CLI for this

task.What is the first step to run management API commands on GAIA's shell?

A. mgmt_admin@teabag > id.txt
B. mgmt_login
C. login user admin password teabag
D. mgmt_cli login user "admin" password "teabag" > id.txt

QUESTION 199

On R80.10 the IPS Blade is managed by:

A. Threat Protection policy
B. Anti-Bot Blade
C. Threat Prevention policy
D. Layers on Firewall policy

Reference:
https://www.checkpoint.com/downloads/product-related/r80.10-mgmt-architecture-overview.pdf

QUESTION 200

When users connect to the Mobile Access portal they are unable to open File Shares.Which log file would you

want to examine?

A. cvpnd.elg
B. httpd.elg
C. vpnd.elg
D. fw.elg

QUESTION 201

What is the correct order of the default "fw monitor" inspection points?

A. i, I, o, O
B. 1, 2, 3, 4
C. i, o, I, O
D. I, i, O, o

QUESTION 202

If an administrator wants to add manual NAT for addresses now owned by the Check Point firewall, what else is
necessary to be completed for it to function properly?

A. Nothing - the proxy ARP is automatically handled in the R80 version
B. Add the proxy ARP configurations in a file called `/etc/conf/local.arp`
C. Add the proxy ARP configurations in a file called `$FWDIR/conf/local.arp`
D. Add the proxy ARP configurations in a file called `$CPDIR/conf/local.arp`

QUESTION 203
Which firewall daemon is responsible for the FW CLI commands?

A. fwd
B. fwm
C. cpm
D. cpd

QUESTION 204

Due to high CPU workload on the Security Gateway, the security administrator decided to purchase a new CPU to replace the existing single core CPU. After installation, is the administrator required to perform any additional tasks?

A. Go to clash-Run cpstop | Run cpstart
B. Go to clash-Run cpconfig | Configure CoreXL to make use of the additional Cores | Exit cpconfig | Reboot Security Gateway
C. Administrator does not need to perform any task. Check Point will make use of the newly installed CPU and Cores
D. Go to clash-Run cpconfig | Configure CoreXL to make use of the additional Cores | Exit cpconfig | Reboot Security Gateway | Install Security Policy

QUESTION 205

GAIA greatly increases operational efficiency by offering an advanced and intuitive software update agent, commonly referred to as the:

A. Check Point Update Service Engine
B. Check Point Software Update Agent
C. Check Point Remote Installation Daemon (CPRID)
D. Check Point Software Update Daemon

QUESTION 206

Hit Count is a feature to track the number of connections that each rule matches, which one is not benefit of Hit Count.

A. Better understand the behavior of the Access Control Policy
B. Improve Firewall performance - You can move a rule that has hot count to a higher position in the Rule Base
C. Automatically rearrange Access Control Policy based on Hit Count Analysis
D. Analyze a Rule Base - You can delete rules that have no matching connections

Reference:

https://sc1.checkpoint.com/documents/R80/CP_R80_SecMGMT/html_frameset.htm?topic=documents/R80/CP_R80_SecMGMT/126197

QUESTION 207

The Check Point history feature in R80 provides the following:

A. View install changes and install specific version
B. View install changes
C. Policy Installation Date, view install changes and install specific version
D. Policy Installation Date only

Reference:

https://sc1.checkpoint.com/documents/R80.10/WebAdminGuides/EN/CP_R80.10_SecurityManagement_AdminG
uide/html_frameset.htm?topic=documents/
R80.10/WebAdminGuides/EN/CP_R80.10_SecurityManagement_AdminGuide/159917

QUESTION 208

No.	Name	Source	Destination	VPN	Services & Applications	Action
1	NetBIOS Noise	* Any	* Any	* Any	NBT	Drop
2	Management	net_10.28.0.0	GW-R7730	* Any	https, ssh	Accept
3	Stealth	* Any	GW-R7730	* Any	* Any	Drop
4	DNS	net_10.28.0.0	* Any	* Any	dns	Accept
5	Web	net_10.28.0.0	* Any	* Any	http, https	Accept
6	DMZ Access	net_10.28.0.0	DMZ_Net_192.0.2.0	* Any	ftp, AP-Defender	Accept
7	Cleanup rule	* Any	* Any	* Any	* Any	Drop

You are the administrator for ABC Corp. You have logged into your R80 Management server. You are making some changes in the Rule Base and notice that rule No.6 has a pencil icon next to it.

What does this mean?

A. This rule No. 6 has been marked for deletion in your Management session.
B. This rule No. 6 has been marked for deletion in another Management session.
C. This rule No. 6 has been marked for editing in your Management session.
D. This rule No. 6 has been marked for editing in another Management session.

QUESTION 209

The back end database for Check Point R80 Management uses:

A. DBMS
B. MongoDB
C. PostgreSQL
D. MySQL

QUESTION 210

UserCheck objects in the Application Control and URL Filtering rules allow the gateway to communicate with the users. Which action is not supported in UserCheck objects?

A. Ask
B. Drop
C. Inform
D. Reject

QUESTION 211

Choose the correct syntax to add a new host named "emailserver1" with IP address 10.50.23.90 using GAiA Management CLI?

A. mgmt_cli add host name "myHost12 ip" address 10.50.23.90
B. mgmt_cli add host name ip-address 10.50.23.90
C. mgmt_cli add host "emailserver1" address 10.50.23.90
D. mgmt_cli add host name "emailserver1" ip-address 10.50.23.90

Reference:

https://weekly-geekly.github.io/articles/339924/index.html

QUESTION 212

SmartConsole R80.x requires the following ports to be open for SmartEvent:

A. 19009, 19090 & 443
B. 19009, 19004 & 18190
C. 18190 & 443
D. 19009, 18190 & 443

QUESTION 213

Which is the correct order of a log flow processed by SmartEvent components?

A. Firewall > Correlation Unit > Log Server > SmartEvent Server Database > SmartEvent Client
B. Firewall > SmartEvent Server Database > Correlation Unit > Log Server > SmartEvent Client
C. Firewall > Log Server > SmartEvent Server Database > Correlation Unit > SmartEvent Client
D. Firewall > Log Server > Correlation Unit > SmartEvent Server Database > SmartEvent Client

QUESTION 214

Which of the following is NOT supported by CPUSE?

A. Automatic download of full installation and upgrade packages
B. Automatic download of hotfixes
C. Installation of private hotfixes
D. Offline installations

Reference:

https://sc1.checkpoint.com/documents/R77/CP_R77_Gaia_AdminWebAdminGuide/html_frameset.htm?topic=doc
uments/R77/_CP_R77_Gaia_AdminWebAdminGuide/112109

QUESTION 215

Aaron is a Cyber Security Engineer working for Global Law Firm with large scale deployment of Check Point
Enterprise Appliances running GaiA R80.X. The Network Security Developer Team is having an issue testing the
API with a newly deployed R80.X Security Management Server. Aaron wants to confirm API services are working
properly. What should he do first?

A. Aaron should check API Server status with "fwm api status" from Expert mode. If services are stopped, he
   should start them with "fwm api start".
B. Aaron should check API Server status with "cpapi status" from Expert mode. If services are stopped, he should
   start them with "cpapi start".
C. Aaron should check API Server status with "api status" from Expert mode. If services are stopped, he should
   start them with "api start".
D. Aaron should check API Server status with "cpm api status" from Expert mode. If services are stopped, he
   should start them with "cpi api start".

QUESTION 216

What is the command to check the status of Check Point processes?

A. top
B. cptop
C. cphaprob list
D. cpws_admin list

Reference:

 https://community.checkpoint.com/t5/General-Management-Topics/cpwd-admin-list-overview-SMS/td-p/29589

QUESTION 217

If SecureXL is disabled which path is used to process traffic?

A. Passive path
B. Medium path
C. Firewall path
D. Accelerated path

QUESTION 218

Installations and upgrades with CPUSE require that the CPUSE agent is up-to-date. Usually the latest build is downloaded automatically. How can you verify the CPUSE agent build?

A. In WebUI Status and Actions page or by running the following command in CLISH: show installer status build
B. In WebUI Status and Actions page or by running the following command in CLISH: show installer status version
C. In the Management Server or Gateway object in SmartConsole or by running the following command in CLISH: show installer status build
D. In the Management Server or Gateway object in SmartConsole or by running the following command in CLISH: show installer agent version

QUESTION 219

When configuring SmartEvent Initial settings, you must specify a basic topology to SmartEvent to help it calculate traffic direction for events. What is this setting called, and what are you defining?

A. Network; and defining your Class A space
B. Topology; and you are defining the Internal network
C. Internal addresses; you are defining the gateways
D. Internal network(s); you are defining your networks

Reference:

https://dl3.checkpoint.com/paid/2f/2f4753f046ea4ee91155a7b7510d8e76/CP_R77_SmartEvent_AdminGuide.pdf?HashKey=1582055588_10a30c668c8356dd47b6e6fa6305c6b4&xtn=.pdf

QUESTION 220

SandBlast offers busineses flexibility in implementation based on their individual business needs. What is an option for deployment of Check Point SandBlast Zero- Day Protection?

A. Smart Cloud Service
B. Any Cloud Service
C. Threat Agent Service
D. Public Cloud Service

QUESTION 221

John detected high load on sync interface. Which is most recommended solution?

A. For FTP connections – do not sync
B. Add a second interface to handle sync traffic
C. For short connections like http service – do not sync
D. For short connections like icmp service – delay sync for 2 seconds

QUESTION 222

Which of the following is NOT an attribute of packet acceleration?

A. Source address
B. Protocol
C. Destination port
D. VLAN tag

Explanation:

Connections are identified by the 5 tuple attributes: source address, destination address, source port, destination port, protocol. When the packets in a connection match all the 5 tuple attributes, the traffic flow can be processed on the accelerated path.

QUESTION 223

Due to high CPU workload on the Security Gateway, the security administrator decided to purchase a new multicore CPU to replace the existing single core CPU. After installation, is the administrator required to perform any additional tasks?

A. Run cprestart from clish
B. After upgrading the hardware, increase the number of kernel instances using cpconfig
C. Administrator does not need to perform any task. Check Point will make use of the newly installed CPU and Cores
D. Hyperthreading must be enabled in the bios to use CoreXL

QUESTION 224

There are 4 ways to use the Management API for creating host object with R80 Management API. Which one is NOT correct?

A. Using Web Services
B. Using cpconfig
C. Using CLISH
D. Using SmartConsole GUI console

QUESTION 225

By default, the R80 web API uses which content-type in its response?

A. Java Script
B. XML
C. Text
D. JSON

QUESTION 226

The "fw monitor" tool can be best used to troubleshoot_________________.

A. Logging issues
B. FWD issues
C. Network traffic issues
D. Authentication issues

Reference:

https://supportcenter.checkpoint.com/supportcenter/portal?eventSubmit_doGoviewsolutiondetails=&solutionid=sk30583

QUESTION 227

What is the best sync method in the ClusterXL deployment?

A. Use 1 cluster + 1st sync
B. Use 1 dedicated sync interface
C. Use 3 clusters + 1st sync + 2nd sync + 3rd sync
D. Use 2 clusters + 1st sync + 2nd sync

QUESTION 228

Kurt is planning to upgrade his Security Management Server to R80.X. What is the lowest supported version of the Security Management he can upgrade from?

A. R76 Splat
B. R77.X Gaia
C. R75 Splat
D. R75 Gaia

QUESTION 229

Which process is used mainly for backward compatibility of gateways in R80.X? It provides communication with GUI-client, database manipulation, policy compilation and Management HA synchronization.

A. cpm
B. fwd
C. cpd
D. fwm

QUESTION 230

According to out of the box SmartEvent policy, which blade will automatically be correlated into events?

A. Firewall
B. VPN
C. IPS
D. HTTPS

QUESTION 231

SmartEvent Security Checkups can be run from the following Logs and Monitor activity:

A. Reports
B. Advanced
C. Checkups
D. Views

QUESTION 232

Which 3 types of tracking are available for Threat Prevention Policy?

A. SMS Alert, Log, SNMP alert
B. Syslog, None, User-defined scripts
C. None, Log, Syslog
D. Alert, SNMP trap, Mail

QUESTION 233

What is the best method to upgrade a Security Management Server to R80.x when it is not connected to the Internet?

A. CPUSE offline upgrade only
B. Advanced upgrade or CPUSE offline upgrade
C. Advanced Upgrade only
D. SmartUpdate offline upgrade

QUESTION 234

Which of the following is NOT a valid type SecureXL template?

A. Accept Template
B. Deny template
C. Drop Template
D. NAT Template

QUESTION 235

Check Point Support in many cases asks you for a configuration summary of your Check Point system. This is also called:

A. cpexport
B. sysinfo
C. cpsizeme
D. cpinfo

ANSWERS

1. Correct Answer: B
2. Correct Answer: D
3. Correct Answer: D
4. Correct Answer: B
5. Correct Answer: B
6. Correct Answer: C
7. Correct Answer: C
8. Correct Answer: B
9. Correct Answer: C
10. Correct Answer: D
11. Correct Answer: C
12. Correct Answer: C
13. Correct Answer: A
14. Correct Answer: A
15. Correct Answer: A
16. Correct Answer: B
17. Correct Answer: B
18. Correct Answer: D
19. Correct Answer: A
20. Correct Answer: D
21. Correct Answer: C
22. Correct Answer: C
23. Correct Answer: D
24. Correct Answer: D
25. Correct Answer: C
26. Correct Answer: C
27. Correct Answer: D
28. Correct Answer: D
29. Correct Answer: B
30. Correct Answer: A
31. Correct Answer: c
32. Correct Answer: B
33. Correct Answer: B
34. Correct Answer: B
35. Correct Answer: D
36. Correct Answer: D
37. Correct Answer: A
38. Correct Answer: A
39. Correct Answer: A
40. Correct Answer: B
41. Correct Answer: C
42. Correct Answer: D
43. Correct Answer: A
44. Correct Answer: D
45. Correct Answer: A
46. Correct Answer: C
47. Correct Answer: B
48. Correct Answer: C
49. Correct Answer: D
50. Correct Answer: B
51. Correct Answer: D
52. Correct Answer: C
53. Correct Answer: B
54. Correct Answer: D

55.	Correct Answer: A
56.	Correct Answer: C
57.	Correct Answer: C
58.	Correct Answer: A
59.	Correct Answer: A
60.	Correct Answer: D
61.	Correct Answer: C
62.	Correct Answer: D
63.	Correct Answer: C
64.	Correct Answer: D
65.	Correct Answer: A
66.	Correct Answer: B
67.	Correct Answer: A
68.	Correct Answer: D
69.	Correct Answer: A
70.	Correct Answer: D
71.	Correct Answer: D
72.	Correct Answer: D
73.	Correct Answer: D
74.	Correct Answer: B
75.	Correct Answer: D
76.	Correct Answer: D
77.	Correct Answer: A
78.	Correct Answer: C
79.	Correct Answer: A
80.	Correct Answer: D
81.	Correct Answer: B
82.	Correct Answer: C
83.	Correct Answer: A
84.	Correct Answer: B
85.	Correct Answer: C
86.	Correct Answer: D
87.	Correct Answer: C
88.	Correct Answer: B
89.	Correct Answer: B
90.	Correct Answer: C
91.	Correct Answer: A
92.	Correct Answer: D
93.	Correct Answer: C
94.	Correct Answer: A
95.	Correct Answer: C
96.	Correct Answer: B
97.	Correct Answer: D
98.	Correct Answer: D
99.	Correct Answer: C
100.	Correct Answer: B
101.	Correct Answer: B
102.	Correct Answer: C
103.	Correct Answer: B
104.	Correct Answer: D
105.	Correct Answer: C
106.	Correct Answer: D
107.	Correct Answer: C
108.	Correct Answer: A
109.	Correct Answer: B
110.	Correct Answer: B
111.	Correct Answer: D
112.	Correct Answer: A
113.	Correct Answer: B

114.	Correct Answer: C
115.	Correct Answer: C
116.	Correct Answer: B
117.	Correct Answer: B
118.	Correct Answer: B
119.	Correct Answer: A
120.	Correct Answer: A
121.	Correct Answer: B
122.	Correct Answer: A
123.	Correct Answer: C
124.	Correct Answer: C
125.	Correct Answer: D
126.	Correct Answer: D
127.	Correct Answer: c
128.	Correct Answer: D
129.	Correct Answer: B
130.	Correct Answer: D
131.	Correct Answer: D
132.	Correct Answer: D
133.	Correct Answer: D
134.	Correct Answer: C
135.	Correct Answer: A
136.	Correct Answer: A
137.	Correct Answer: C
138.	Correct Answer: D
139.	Correct Answer: C
140.	Correct Answer: A
141.	Correct Answer: D
142.	Correct Answer: A
143.	Correct Answer: C
144.	Correct Answer: B
145.	Correct Answer: D
146.	Correct Answer: B
147.	Correct Answer: C
148.	Correct Answer: D
149.	Correct Answer: C
150.	Correct Answer: B
151.	Correct Answer: B
152.	Correct Answer: D
153.	Correct Answer: C
154.	Correct Answer: C
155.	Correct Answer: B
156.	Correct Answer: A
157.	Correct Answer: B
158.	Correct Answer: D
159.	Correct Answer: B
160.	Correct Answer: B
161.	Correct Answer: D
162.	Correct Answer: A
163.	Correct Answer: AD
164.	Correct Answer: D
165.	Correct Answer: A
166.	Correct Answer: B
167.	Correct Answer: B
168.	Correct Answer: D
169.	Correct Answer: A
170.	Correct Answer: B
171.	Correct Answer: C
172.	Correct Answer: A

173.	Correct Answer: A
174.	Correct Answer: C
175.	Correct Answer: A
176.	Correct Answer: C
177.	Correct Answer: D
178.	Correct Answer: B
179.	Correct Answer: A
180.	Correct Answer: B
181.	Correct Answer: B
182.	Correct Answer: A
183.	Correct Answer: A
184.	Correct Answer: A
185.	Correct Answer: D
186.	Correct Answer: A
187.	Correct Answer: B
188.	Correct Answer: A
189.	Correct Answer: A
190.	Correct Answer: B
191.	Correct Answer: B
192.	Correct Answer: A
193.	Correct Answer: B
194.	Correct Answer: B
195.	Correct Answer: D
196.	Correct Answer: C
197.	Correct Answer: B
198.	Correct Answer: B
199.	Correct Answer: C
200.	Correct Answer: A
201.	Correct Answer: C
202.	Correct Answer: C
203.	Correct Answer: A
204.	Correct Answer: B
205.	Correct Answer: A
206.	Correct Answer: C
207.	Correct Answer: C
208.	Correct Answer: C
209.	Correct Answer: C
210.	Correct Answer: D
211.	Correct Answer: D
212.	Correct Answer: D
213.	Correct Answer: D
214.	Correct Answer: D
215.	Correct Answer: C
216.	Correct Answer: D
217.	Correct Answer: C
218.	Correct Answer: A
219.	Correct Answer: D
220.	Correct Answer: D
221.	Correct Answer: A
222.	Correct Answer: D
223.	Correct Answer: B
224.	Correct Answer: B
225.	Correct Answer: D
226.	Correct Answer: C
227.	Correct Answer: B
228.	Correct Answer: D
229.	Correct Answer: D
230.	Correct Answer: C
231.	Correct Answer: A

232.   Correct Answer: B
233.   Correct Answer: B
234.   Correct Answer: B
235.   Correct Answer: D